The Apple Star

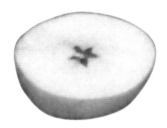

by Cecilia Cortés

photographs by Adrian Heke

Learning Media

I like red apples.

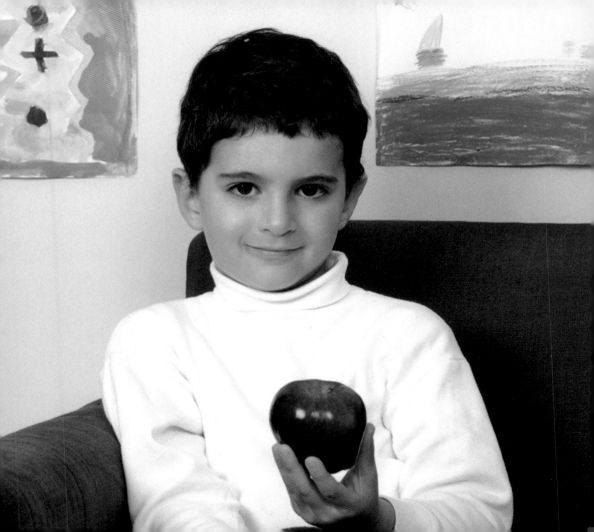

I like green apples.

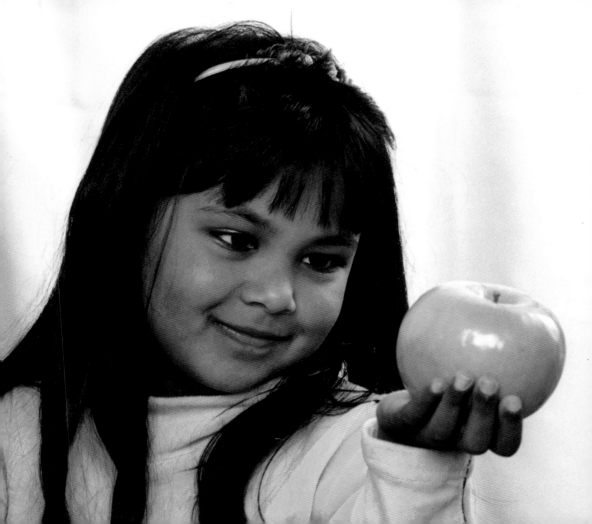

I like yellow apples.

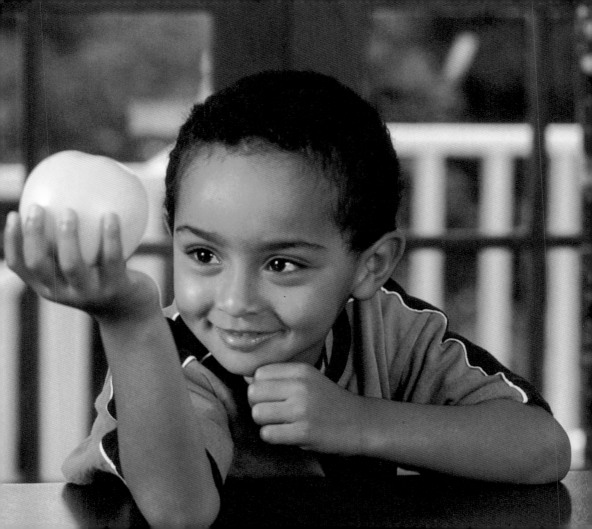

I like apple pie.

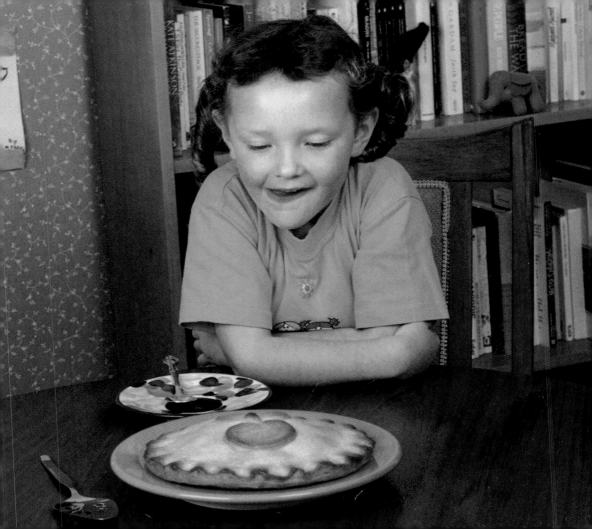

I like apple sauce.

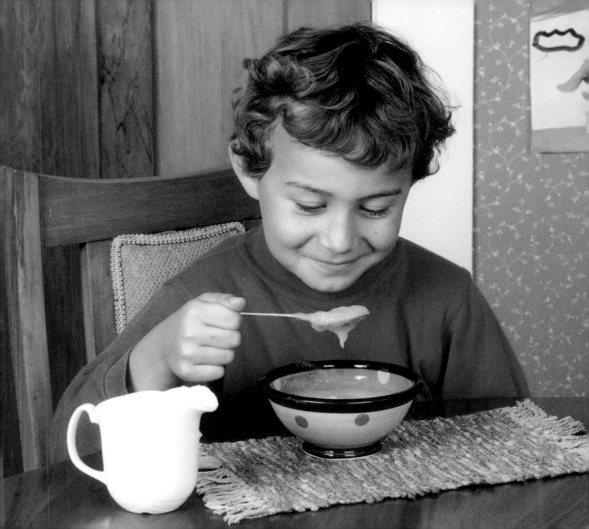

I like apple cake.

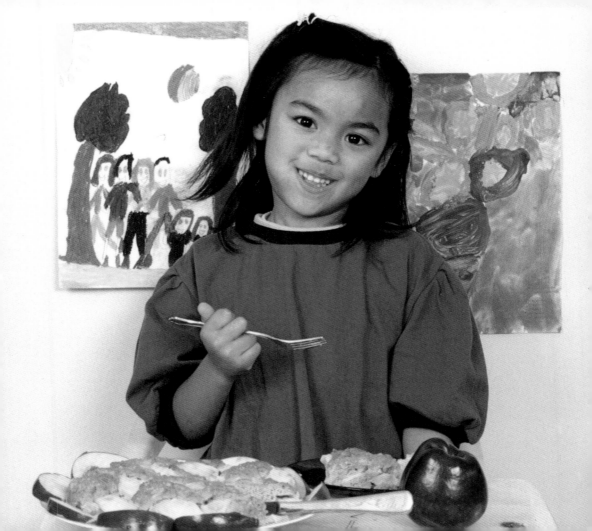

I like apple jelly.

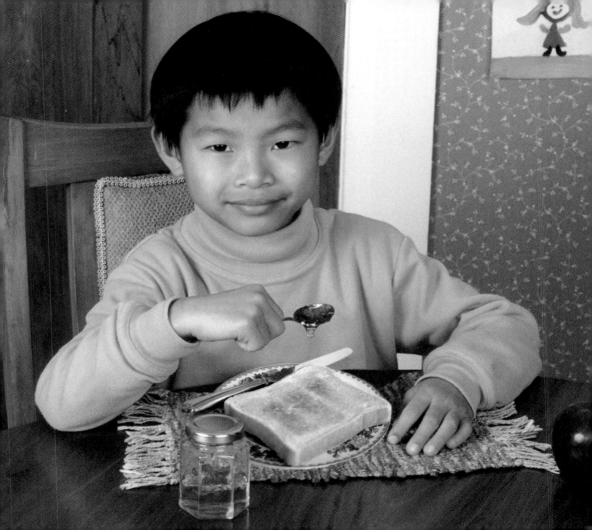

We like the apple star!

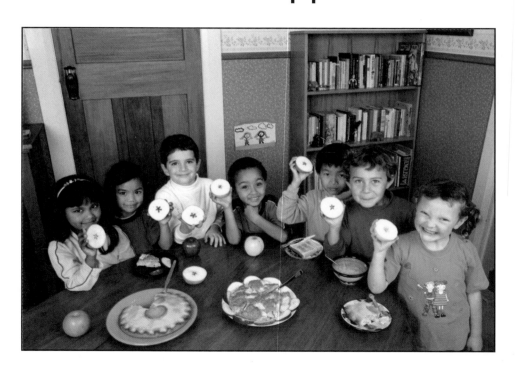